How to Feel Confident
with Your Special Talents

How to Feel Confident with Your Special Talents

Carol Guess & Daniela Olszewska

Black
Lawrence
Press

www.blacklawrence.com

Executive Editor: Diane Goettel
Book and Cover Design: Amy Freels
Cover Art: *Old Bermuda Inn, Staten Island, New York* by Corinne May Botz

Published 2014 by Black Lawrence Press.
Printed in the United States.

Contents

How to Do the Cha Cha

Stay alert in red rolling light. Focus premium-like in 4/4 time. Go into debt with arms held in minor Jezebel pose. Small sidestep about the star specks on the floor. Chin up during the landslide. Sexy bend, sexy bend! Practice—

Perfect understanding of where your partner is coming from. Your partner is coming from the same revolutionary party you came from. Don't go about this the wrong way again. Or the next gala will find you cowering under a punch bowl, strained cheek rouged up in-

Panic-rose.

Boys and girls in panic rows. Roadkill of the Rodeo, toeing the party line on one side of the fault line, quaking. Which side are you on, lead or follow-fallow?

Push; no, pull. Adjust your slippery straps and swaddle sandals in bandages: it's open season on open-toed slip-ons. Lesson: don't leave *cha* to chance. Change into a tux and bind yourself into a seamless Mister. Move her, Master Manipulator.

Sway the small of her back with your small, gloved hand.

How to Cheat at Poker

Paint your toenails in the shade of mirror. Wear open-ended shoes. Glint with the best of them. Move to Kansas City. Pop out of a cake. Wearing thirteen flavors of frosting. Your hair teased all heiress-like.

Vouch for the jacks. When you know someone who knows someone with chips. Substitute an accent; exaggerate a cough. Get high and mighty up in the prescription medicine aisle. Stay in your long sleeves and multiple pockets. Fold prettily. An origami made into luck.

Wear photos of strange children in a locket that dangles off-angle. Lean into stranger danger. Take wrong ones to bed. Mornings, demand a pastry case wheeled into your room by a bevy of showgirls. Hide kings and aces in plumes and pasties. Burn anything evidence. Bury the key.

Leave no luck to chance. Change cities and dogs. Tiptoe down stairways and listen, rouged rogue. Get caught up with red hands. Learn faint-sway. Learn slipknot and slideknot. Learn a different lesson from the one they try and teach you. Make bank.

How to Take Action when You Lose Sight of Your Child at an Amusement Park

Ferret out the Ferris wheel, sherbet orange and pickle green. Fall into line, lockstepping. Cutting in line breeds violence. Kid has other father's eyes, other father's ginger tangles. He lives here now, a homespun school.

Ride that sugar high before you hightail it to the Sit 'n Spin. Vibrating pocket, ICE on the line. Kid wandered off, Kid wants what we all want. You're a shelter of feral cats clawing bars on a rickety roller. Stuffed banana or deep-friend dough?

It's always twilight in the Tunnel of Love. Glide your boat through a flotilla of kissers. Water seeps into your high top sneakers. If he was yours, you'd know.

Mister, have you seen my baby? It has a Tilt-a-Whirl curl atop its head. And a troublesome snaggle of a smile. What kind of child runs towards a bearded lady's corpse? And if it's just an optical illusion, why not say so outright?

What we mean is, this place was better when it was 18 and up.

Now, though, everyone is getting more and more carnie. After hours of superhero-themed joyrides, the insides get scrambled to the point. You don't have to think about things like feelings anymore. Paint a planet on your cheek. Turn the other cheek! Paint a different planet, one with a lot of rings.

How to Climb a Ladder Safely

Here we are at skybottom, wearing house slippers outside the house because it is already so summer that we can get away with anything.

Here we are at a palm tree, staring up at one black and six-toed cat, waiting for the fire department to show up and coax because this is what always happened on Saturday morning TV.

Here we are taking the long way around the ladder because avoidance actually cures superstition.

Here we are, three rungs up, flashing back to Florida.

Here we are, changing places. I'm up top and you're below. When we get to the middle, one of us dangles.

Undress me on a ladder and my legs look longer.

Rats are clever ladder-makers. They climb vines, sills, and pipes to reach rooftops and shimmy through shingles.

Here we are, peering out at the wreckage. Mourning those we knew and those we didn't.

Here I am and here you are, "we" dissolving on the slow climb down. Violet twilight, bruising light.

You saw off the top rung.

Here we are, tossing coins to make decisions.

How to Dress for a Ouija Board Session

Try to go with a dress that is very fancy and old-fashioned. Think whorehouse madam with a side of zombie. Maiden aunt touched up or down in the style of Edward Gorey. If you don't have a fancy dress, go with a bathrobe.

Put on some gloves and a scarf. Or lots of jewelry. Or tattoo a Celtic cross between your white heavings.

Wear a belt if it would look good with your dress. Tip: A belt will probably not look good with a bathrobe. Even if its buckle is made of a dead elephant's trunk.

Put on a dramatic amount of make-up. Pile your hair on top of your head. Paint your nails black; paint the living room purple. Didn't you leave your cup by the sink?

Hum a song from childhood. Notice that nothing seems to be where you left it. The curtains sway, although there is no breeze. Lost socks reappear in the dryer. Lipstick smooches the mirror: Crème Peach.

What's more surprising: fake real or real fake? Put down the board. You won't be needing that now. You're alone with three vowels and a henna tattoo. Consonants skitter into corners, unused.

How to Calculate the Value of Scrap Gold

Gold prices tend to rise along with worries of war or inflation. Your gold is hiding in so many places: In mafia teeth. In heart-shape. In time, in pocket, in watch form. In shoe bomb and car bomb. In cross. In pavement. In California hills. In princess bed. In fort. In world's most expensive dessert. In pseudo-Egyptian.

The best way to weigh a melted antique locket is to weigh yourself first, then swallow the gold. Weigh yourself again. Feel the gold nugget nudging girlparts.

A golden bullet will neither kill nor injure a werewolf. The only things that will survive the nuclear holocaust are werewolves, cockroaches, and the gold standard. And maybe you, if you finance right.

Dig deep enough inside. You own the money shot, the gold erection. When adding or subtracting, remember to always carry the one. Most scrap gold dealers keep the calculation a secret.

How to Earn a Legitimate Living Working from Home

Show up late to work, eyes foggy with datenight. Play Watercooler Gossip at the kitchen sink. Be big boss with snappy tone and fingersnaps. Hold meeting on couch; nap.

Sexually harass yourself. Throw papers in air; arrange fallen-style. Check: company email, work email, personal email, old personal email, secret email. Write memos to self. Lunch.

Put the dancing on in front of the mirror your computer has become. Pet computer-pet. Listen sympathetically to computer-BFF. She lives in Japan, thinks you are friends with Lindsay Lohan.

Surf house porn, personal ads, job ads, headlines, gossip sites, stocks. Cute animals rescued from icy ponds.

Stare out smudged window at billowy tree, douche ad or Roman Polanski movie.

Heart yourself in bathroom graffiti. Run out of toilet paper. Trip to the store, blinded by real-time light, real-time people, moving cars, strollers, banana peels, parallel parking, and government shutdown.

Prearrange for a cab. Sit for three minutes and sixteen seconds. Pretend this is an urban environment.

Walk up five flights of stairs, then down. Arms overhead: company gym. Work it, baby.

Acknowledge failure to thrive, lapsed Apgar, loneliness. No runway walks. Write day's document in twenty minutes.

Beat yourself over your own deadhorsehead with a copy of *The Fountainhead*. Do this after you've given up the idea of taking up drinking again. Consider bleaching the hair on your arms.

Buy a pink slip. Wear it insideout on Casual Friday. Stand outside your office door and chant UNION, UNION, UNION. Anonymously tip off the Feds. And the reporters. Use one of those little machines that scrambles your natural speaking voice into a zombie robot voice.

Map out ideas for pyramid schemes. Call yourself a bottom and a top. An entrepreneur with a dash of gumdrop dew. Then, frame a picture of a timecard and hang it up somewhere. Frame a picture of an hourglass and put it away in a drawer somewhere. Feel something like shame, but less acute.

This is the yourtimeisnow time for a break, a benefit, a raise, a postal-level freakout. This is yourtimetoshine. In junior executive suites. In pink tweed careerwear. You are truly modern, you are massively productive.

How to Donate Your Body to Science

1.

Start with a flesh wound. Add 2 lbs. of agnostic-in-a-bag. Stir in an existential neck cord. Look good naked.

No relations, save an eccentrically-coiffed great aunt in Minneapolis. Left a lot of lovers but none so close as to want your toe tag ticket. Missed more than a few slow buses.

2.

For some people, making a contribution to society doesn't stop with their death.

For some people, making a contribution to society only starts with their death.

3.

I roomed with a girl from Grand Rapids; she was an organ donor. Or, a potential one. She had signed the back of her license. But she specified that the only organs they could take were her liver and her lungs. She hoped they would go to someone who didn't deserve them, she said. Someone who got cancer through dumb life choices rather than dumb bad luck. When this girl found out that my dad was a truck driver, she started telling people that her dad was a truck driver. Her dad wasn't a truck driver, he was in some kind of business. I don't know, I never know what people's dads do.

She slept in the nude, a thin sheet for cover. Once the sheet slipped. I marked potential donations with circles and arrows. When she woke up, it wasn't funny. She left to visit her boyfriend, who I'd slept with twice because he had A/C. That night she didn't come back at all. This was pre-Interweb, pre-Googling "accident" and "Jennifer Pratt." Every siren made me think of the taste of her stomach when I licked her skin.

How to Avoid Leaving DNA at a Scene or How to Descend a Staircase Gracefully

Do the dirty deed.

Do it like you planned it. For a black and white photo-op.

Set a small fire for the smell of singed crosshair. Affect an air of eccentric. Wear a peignoir trimmed in Siamese cattails.

You are a bump off doll with a sweet safecracker. Clam shut, dame-dish. The lowdown is you're about to get clipped anyway.

Tiptoe, socked soles slippery-subtle. Sock it to time-lapse, camera cracked. Think of the catwalk, pivot and moue. Lean into lean time, banister-width. Ladyfingers sparkling with diamond dust.

Gloves finger shadow government. Some agents of holy hardboiled Hollywood.

Perfume lingers in the hop-room. Trail neither gardenia nor milkshake-musk. You are a model descending the stair. You are a role model. You model roles. You must not be seen in public cavorting with wrong people; fuck wrong people; pleasure yourself.

O, you are a straight shooter, all right.

Swipe dust with skirt scrim. Think snood, braids saddled in faux pearl swaddle. Breathe into blouson cleavage crease.

::::: ^^^^^ running from scene of crime; hiding in forest

%%{}%% lying to police while wearing form-fitting sheath

How to Use the Hungarian Algorithm

Get minimum-matching. Put the people on the left, the variables on the right. Raise your hand high to the fluorescent-flecked ceiling. Matrix evenly, don't mix the numbers. Remember, rows will shift if you let them alone for too long; consider employing a small whip or spider-teeth-sharp spurs to keep everything on the upandup. Mix in beet-based nutrients. Strong bones are necessary for the tasks ahead. Grind up a fractal or three and throw them over your shoulder. This is lite superstition, but even arithmetic must make allowances for high romance.

I knew a polymath with a pocket protector but no pens or pencil to protect the pocket from. There was another who had spent a year in the Soviet Union. Some pre-calculus was always giving the thinner, quieter boys rides out to the golf courses in the suburbs. Computer cards were calling cards. Professor X scrawled equations in frost, scribbled solutions on cloth napkins in restaurants. Some part of his big-buttoned brain was always working, even sleeping or tending to hygiene. When an answer came, he'd glaze. My body fell away. Only numbers were beautiful then. I could never match their perfection.

By now you've guessed: I was his mistress. Once he left me at the country club. I spent the night feasting on crumbs, sipping frothy drinks left by stumbling wait staff. I waited for X but he never came back; that's what the dead do: don't.

Don't say math is stupid, say you're too sexy to understand it. Don't roll your tongue off the solve-for-r part of the equation.

How to Tell the Difference Between Nerds and Geeks

Difficulty with voice modulation. Counselor reports a natural inclination towards toned-but-pasty form. Won reptiles or goldfish at county fair, but they're long-dead from neglect. At least one uncle accused of white collar crime. Wears contacts. Travels to Egypt. Keeps a boyfriend or a girlfriend but isn't very nice to him/her. Because there are many kinds of comfort. Wars on the Interweb, on the dance floor, on the backs of the people who inhabit the ads inside the comic books. Knows everything about one or two things. Recognizes signs of fiefdom in pretty much the entire western world. Gargles Diet Mountain Dew in the midst of professional puberty crisis.

Trouble with emoticon morale. Phys ed instructor reports spaghetti limbs, stuck together. Owns cute kitten; refers to it as Cute Kitten. At least one cousin is a famous comedian. Rocks galoshes. Hikes Graveyards of the western States. Moonlights as a dominatrix but isn't very good with pliers. Because there are many kinds of pain. Rules the internet and comic book sales. Knows everything about intellectual crush. Recognizable thumbprint whorls in pretty much the entire library. Drinks diet soda in the midst of drunken cohort's revelry.

How to Ensure No One Argues when Playing Princess Party Games or How to Stop Misbehaving in Public

Come party time, be sure entertainment is age-appropriate. Adults will laugh at anything involving sex, children will laugh at cartoon characters sustaining minor injuries. Consider merging these comedic genres. Alternatively, consider separating the women from the girls via industrial strength butterfly nets.

Scrub your mouth out with bubblesoft. Use your new waterboard on yr mom's waterbed. Stuff with cupcakes instead of cake. A second color/flavor of frosting instead of sprinkles. Not everyone can be a princess. Not everyone gets dishes monogrammed in dainty gold HRH. But the right half of a diadem can get you up to the cloudgate.

If you're wearing the wrong half, it's about time to get amusing yourself. Get a little bit anorexic, like the opposite of getting a little bit pregnant again. Write a twelve-page holiday letter describing the accomplishments of your imaginary children, include upcoming film/TV appearances. Direct a one-act play called *Kitchen*. Stamp thank-you notes at intermission. Construct a lawn sculpture titled "Temptation in Pink." (mittens hinder hand temptation, tube socks hinder shin temptation, blinders hinder porn temptation—)
Make sure there is no actual pink in the sculpture.

How to Avoid Overstimulation or How to Reattach Plastic Lettering to a Jersey

Down suburbs, Chrissy locked me in the panic room with a bottle of Nair and *The Joy of Cooking*. Or *The Joy of Sex*. I was learning Confection. How to Sculpt Pastry from Singed Hair and Bone.

She wasn't the boss of me. We lettered in Splay, French manicures tumescent in our experimentation with color, light, gesture. We bound each other's wrists with phone cords stretched rec room to porch. All split level-with-an-attitude, enemies trudging in the same direction. Our parents divorced the city, shoving horses aside. Pimping out the countryside.

Minus traffic we were promised quiet, but cereal echoed and socks shuffled static. Birds chirped like horns honking Stop 'n Go.

She taught me shave, prank, pink. I taught her uplift, binder, thinner. We BFF'd phone numbers with paperclips and magic markers.

Some post-prom return to the city this is, Chrissy, Chrissy. Now, let me out of the sitting room. I'm too oranged with Sun-In and *Our Bodies, Ourselves*. You unlearnt me. Look at this Spice Rack. How to Rearrange The 2000 Years Worth of Salt. Your idea of a graduation present surprises me in half.

But I'll lead you around now. I've still got my jacket for Ditching Homeroom and Scrawling Minor Female Obscenities on the Walls of the Rectory. On the orphan-track, soon we'll measure in city blocks, leather-elbowed w/clouding over a good third of our pout-face.

A cockroach-induced breakthrough leads to a calm hand holding over a hospital bed. To think she would be the one to grow up to not be able to deal . . . I read her the day's riot acts; I stretch out the post-prom gloves in hopes that she wasn't still the boss of me.

How to Avoid Suspicion and Paranoia

1. Start with a forest fire

2. Hidden meaning hiding out from you

3. All these pervs living in the same school district

4. The salt pig's cracked from since before I can remember

5. And devolve into specifically Anglo-type distrust

6. Don't tonic me, you mofo in a government-themed dress

7. Transitioning from bad to worse

8. Skinny jean is the new distressed denim

9. A twenty tucked into the waistband of my wife

10. Foreclose distraction with polka-dot piping

11. Redistricting my Facebook friends

12. You are part of the problematizing formula, privatize houseplants

13. I spiked the canteens

14. Dressing room cameras discourage sex and shoplifting

15. Unpack solutions to genetically-modified filibusters

16. Behind my back, there are a thousand and one nights

17. Ghost town real estate license

18. When you said you knew me from before, I didn't realize

19. That you meant before as in back in Colorado

20. Let's go about whistleblowing while we work

How to Make a Meal of One Color or How to Stop Coworkers from Stealing Your Food

O ruinous lip prints! O ruinous other-smudges staining Styrofoam cups! O strawberries! O French fries dipped in ketchup! O killer tomato from outer space! O movie theater floor Twizzlers! O snakefruit! O radicalized cherries, post-picking + in season! O scolding Soviet grandmother's borscht! O quivering veal on a paper plate!

Tie bib around neck, fold napkin to Bargain Birthday Bouquet. Punch time clock with toast. At noon + 1, hasten to shared company fridge and rummage through moldy last month's snacks. Find yr tidy yogurt and crackers. Spread embroidered napkin at desk, tuck napkin on lap. Smear antibacterial chemicals on fingers, food, keyboard, shoe soles, doorknob.

Hey now, there's the dress code, and then there's the. dress. code.

Water fountain wears new necklace: *This water has been tested for lead. Less than maximum contamination levels were found. Enjoy drinking here.* Also, in water closet: *Washing hands increases company productivity by 12%.*

Fridays are casual cubetime: hoedown in jeans and plaid plackets, but no kilts for men or g-strings peeking out from mom jeans. How to Manage Yr Cleavage at Work = six pages of drawings sculpting what's showable and what's a showgirl.

Live in fear of absently saying Iloveyou instead of Haveaniceday. It's less awkward when it happens on the phone. But still, the cold calling sometimes leaves things open for after hours.

O meaty sandwich smear left in shared microwave! O sad sack noodle dish everyone eats for cheapness! O smelly takeout from bad deli that sickens someone sometimes! O bulimic intern vomiting on the clock! O curdling in the back of the communal cupboard! O sales rep luncheon leftovers from before the merger!

Be a secret shopper, then. Be a food critic, for all I care.

How to Remember a Person's Name

Aphasia it: Here's Mr. Teal and Mr. Soapflake with their friend Mr. Mambo. And there's Ms. Orange Bitters and the Misses Softgrass.

Turn it inside out: John becomes Ohjn. Or, if he's a particularly unpleasant fellow, Honj. Another option is to flip it backwards. This works best for lefthanders.

Your pleather pocketbook sequesters numbers crumpled on napkins: initials slurred to inksmear, lipstick prints, an exclamation mark after Call me. The best thing to do in this situation is wait three days for a sign. Call after midnight. Ask for Odette.

If someone's face reminisces alphabets, daub butter on teatime bread. Waking up with a stranger is no problem at all! Practice murmuring nothing with poise. Whisper consonants into morningtime coffee, all S romantical.

Embroider nicknames. Soft-shoe spell blocks. If you forget your own name, christen another. Former cheerleaders may find it helpful to forage their cheerbanks for random results.

How to Be a Good Neighbor

Being on bad terms with your neighbor can make your life slag like a coalmine canary. So be sure to put some calligraphy font on your welcome mat. If you are missing the point, the classic homemade pie never fails once you consider your neighbor's lifestyle. Contribute to discussions about the lawn ornaments with strobe lights. If it gets too loud, they shouldn't hesitate to let you know. Be aware of shared walls, of feminine wiles, and how often you wear high heels. Avoid slamming doors. Stir sugar and share some. Howl first. Floss, fence, retreat. If their mailbox sags with forgone foreclosure, fatten your skort with snail mail and shred. Don't look when they peep thru their fireproof curtains. Let begonias be bygones. Trap, neuter, release.

How to Make People Think You're Immortal

Easiest to lie in the late afternoon. To fool others, start by fooling yourself.
Mail mail to your door in a stranger's strange font, written on parchment
(card stock soaked in tea).

Forge silver dagger to use as letter opener. Plop down in plush rug. Read
with crow-heavy and credulous eyes.

In the letter, learn that you were an experimental child; that is,
experimented upon. They tied you to a bed and injected you with
Everlastingness. One of ten; cohort unknown.

You get to getting aware of your black and blue blood thickened with
batwing and/or turpentine. Lumps that bulge outside-in. Body that works
in nightshift. Before, you rented a new room every four or five months.

Now you sell shoes at a store in the mall. Not dying's expensive, so you
shoplift at lunch. Nights, baby bird, you open your mouth. Gems sparkle
up from your gut like a city.

After a long time, you started to consider the question of passing.

Fall for a girl whose hair smells like pretzels. Tell the truth: this is the least
complex thing about you. Throw fully-cooked rice when she marries some
mortal so birds won't ingest uncooked kernels and die.

How to Be Friends With a Lesbian

Two girls fight over a cabbage in the market. They tear its leaves out one by one.

This is the same place hedgehogs come from. When they were little, you kept them about your person.

Pockets are just holes with safety nets sewn in.

So much for the blushing bite.

Anyone can thread a needle. A rich man living in Tent City is indistinguishable from his tent.

I think I might be the poor man's double entendre.

Love is the most overused abstraction, the alphabet's version of pastel blue.

Dip in, dip out. How to spasm with the library + such floating over your head?

Dancing With the Stars is cute, but do you have to do it outside my room?

The frequency gets set up to solar eclipse.

Reality TV is nothing new. People have been peeping since the serpent snaked the garden.

Thank you for your support.

I understand how plumbing works. You root around under the house.
Come up with dirty boots.

With a Venus smear on the bottom of the right sole.

How to Laugh Naturally on Cue

Shake funny bones from the belly up. Quivering piano in yr jowls. This is
not a test. Amuse me or I'll fire.

As a child I was for children on a small stage. We clapped on cue,
mouths parted, painted silver, braces monstrous as our appetite
for metal.

Think whatever gets you through the night—animals dressed in people
clothes, people dressed in animal skins—incongruity is always funny.
Unless it's uncomfortable, then it's hilarious.

No one followed me home. I shut the door and swallowed the key.
Later, grown-up, I was alone in an alley until someone joined me.

Kill a clown. Kill a hundred clowns. Don't remember where you hid their
bodies. Because their bodies dissolved into puddles of red cotton candy.

A little bit of a clown isn't uncomfortable; only the expansion of
clowns, frizzed hair making trees of opportunities for laughter.

Highball your voice. Sound less innocent; crunch piano keys between
tooth gaps.

There's nothing to regret about a small car or a dog with a
sequined collar.

Clowns are neither people nor animals.

How to Deal With People Who Insist That Something Is Bothering You when Nothing Is Really Wrong

No one understands trees, having listened exclusively to people for so long. Birds resist remote control. Smiles shoulder the burden for others. You're neither < nor > teams.

Take this memo as a token of my affection.

No one is stupid unless you cast them adrift.

Above you, very tall people (metaphorically speaking) believe in their own power and cast you into a pit w/ lions.

To watch another person stumble and take their elbow and help them cross the street and go into the drugstore with them and help them purchase aspirin (which is on sale and may be taken daily to prevent something dire, although not in children under the age of ten) makes sense in your worldview, rather than setting said stumbler adrift and calling them stupid or underneath.

People fly planes that reach beyond what birds could even be interested in. But this is not necessarily smart.

Who will wipe your chin?

Who will tuck back the tag sticking out from above your collar?

Try not to be the kind of stranger who gets offended when girls don't smile. It's nothing personal, it's political. Like a cartoon of a radish wearing a moustache stabbing itself repeatedly with a fork.

So quit barking, *Smile! You're beautiful!* Seems nice-gestured and gentleman-worthy, but, really, it's a creep cracking into someone else's face and you should know better by now.

There are better ways to coax someone out of a nosebleed. Don't go around demanding what should come natural, in the course of this peace you are making here inside the earth. We are bound in this garden dust, let's not make it worse by asking too much.

How to Tolerate Working with Obnoxious People or How to Perform a Simple Leap Over Stairs

Coworkers are constellations dominating daylight stars. A little fainting at the water fountain. A little party you alone were not invited to:

party favor

party hat

Smile, like falling, the same rushed feeling. There are rules for everything:

1. Nametags over right breast, not left, in case of flash mob pledge of allegiance.

2. Hours clearly posted on government-issue office door; office carpet as ugly as possible; no political messages on door or window, including forehead and chest if forehead and chest are pressed to window. Jumping out of window is considered a political message and is therefore forbidden.

3. Memos should be as long as possible. The longer the memo, the more important it is. Put important part of memo at the end of the memo, preferably condensed into one or two sentences.

4. Flowers and fruit baskets are sent to coworkers when:

a. biological father has died and coworker is not gay

b. baby has been birthed and neither coworker nor baby are gay

c. coworker looks pale due to office diet tips gone viral

d. coworker is on Special Committee Advising Special Administrator to the Special Seat of Special Extras

5. Refreshments shall consist of: the same box of vanilla cookies without frosting or other adornment; half a pot of coffee; hot water; loose tea. Meetings shall be called to order by the first person whose tea leaves form an X in the bottom of their paper cup.

6. Employees with children or nieces and nephews should feel free to leave order forms for wrapping paper and Girl Scout cookies on Management's desk.

7. Each department will pick a woman to hold in mistrust and contempt. Label her hopelessly stupid. Prone to wardrobe and grammar errors. Use shared mistrust and contempt to engender feelings of "community," or, in more advanced departments, "family."

8. Pick another woman to regard in horror. Label her hopelessly slutty. Prone to discretion and web-surfing errors. Use shared horror to engender feelings of "family," or, in more advanced departments, "love."

9. Proper small talk with coworkers is pretty much limited to:
    a. normal sports (normal, as defined by location and season—hockey, for example, is normal in Michigan, in winter, but not in Georgia in the spring)
    b. adventures in commuting
    c. latest stupid thing woman (see 7) or slutty thing woman (see 8) did
    d. speculation as to when the photocopier will get repaired

10. All employees should consider attending the mandatory meeting with the PR firm. In the event of an emergency, leaps of faith should be kept to a minimum. We look forward to responding to your queries.

How to Overcome Procrastination Using Self Talk

Wrapped up in lazy floral patterns, it's difficult to care about the small mammal demised in the space between your 1st story ceiling and your 2nd story floor. The landlord doesn't want to rip through architecture. He pumps mummifying gas into the space you can't reach. The place smells of funeral home, but it's better than the smell of real decay.

Nights, mammal kin congregate in the space between, the space of witness, now poisonous gas. You hear their procession, tiptoeing the body back to where they came from. Iced-over fields, thawing to spring.

50 student essays on the reverse racism of gay abortions. Leave the coffee and the open flame. Leave the jerking hand by the stack of papers in hopes of an act of God, an excuse from grading on the grounds of a technicality. Run.

Do not run. You are going to the frozen yogurt store, where all the running would get undone. Instead, surf eBay for new running shoes. Get outbid by moxiegurl7878. Remember that your ex went by "moxiegurl" when you met, and lived at 17878 Maple Leaf Way.

Put your old shoes on the front mat, as you did when you were small, hoping someone will fill them with candy. Instead shoes fill with feet, with mud, with miles to walk before you finish grading, before this job leads to the next, and the next.

Fall asleep with your face against the frozen yogurt, forehead stuck to nutritional chart. Wake when your spoon clatters onto the floor. Check on your sneakers in high hopes of candy. Instead, baby mice: thumb-sized, divine.

How to Get an Egg Into a Bottle or How to Act at a Funeral

A duck and a dragon sever the Easter basket in the sixth stage of photosynthesis. You're noticeably less impressed. This ball of flame in a cloudbox would make a decent second act.

Sunday they firebombed the house Houdini got born through. None of the mirrors so much as cracked. His ghost wants chains and circus back.

O audience of captive kin

O rising lilies, soft as smoke

O doves released on store-bought cards

O diminishing tree, dead on the corner where the driver, distracted, changed the CD

We're matching mother-daughter cutlery in honor of the Christ capture. We're scrambling what's left outside the bottle. You chip a tooth on embalmed egg.

Music follows us from nave to have not. May the dead tree's birds grow back.

How to Draw an Accurate Mental Map of the World

Pencil in a sea for every pirate song in the key of E flat.

Explain the differences between saltwater and freshwater.

Compass the northwest.

Compare Atlantis, Titanic, and dolphins trained to kiss on the mouth.

There ain't no mountain high enough.

Figure in for the glacial problem.

Some plate sliding is to be expected.

Ditto renaming post-revolution.

Old maps reveal xenophobia, racism, and religious bias; new maps reveal economic inequalities.

       Q: Are these the same thing?

Some alien abductors require more troops than others.

If you google your own location, you'll go blind.

Shadow government headquarters don't appear on any map. They have their own maps and mapmakers, and their own DJs for parties.

If you steal from a mapmaker, he/she will erase your address from the maps he/she makes. Your location will be represented as a fire hydrant or a waste treatment plant.

Mermaids have scales covering girl parts; otherwise, fake mermaids (hoax).

Hide the information in the Freud-made part of your brain.

Blame tsunami on president of Judas Priest fan club.

When in doubt, label all the capitals Providence City.

A: Africa is bigger than you think it is.

How to Ride an Icelandic Horse

Get on a plane. Arrive in Iceland. Discover that Icelandic horses are fuzzy and fussy, and live in red barns. They graze for hours, draped in blue blankets. Horses in their dreams are clouds.

Pet your Icelandic horse gently. Call it "Sigrid" or "Astrid." Feed it some hay.

And neigh at the clouds in the pre-thunderstorm afternoon. A kerchief full of carrots, sugar cubes, and tranquilizers and you're scout-level prepared. Hum towards the hillsides—you've already escaped the wrong end of the fairy tale stick, what's left to frown at?

Get on a plane. Fly back to your American town, minus Icelandic horse. Go to the mall. Buy sneakers that light up when you run. A red candle that smells like the potpourri of the innkeeper's underthings drawer.

Miss horse. Draw countless pictures of horses at work. At play, at placid concentration of very green field, at escape from glue factory, and/or at jumping show with fancy bridle. Explain to your coworkers that you speak Icelandic. Respond to "Sigrid," "Astrid," or "Giddy." Do not respond to "Becky" or "John."

Stretch your ears and nose and, mostly, your neck. Brand your left butt cheek. And your right one too, it's good measure. Take to sleeping standing up in your office manager's two-car garage.

Be secretly pleased when your friends and coworkers stage a 12-step style intervention for you. Listen patiently while they read aloud from their prepared statements. They feel like they don't even know who you are anymore, baby.

Peruse brochures for treatment facilities out in Arizona—they look nice, actually, most of them have vaguely Native American-sounding names. So much progress has been made over the past few years. Promising new treatments. Nothing like what it used to be, back in your mother's day.

Smile in grace-time, open your mouth to explain the situation as it really is, as the opposite of what these people in the room think, as, here, the thing is, you really are an Icelandic horse. Snort and whinny. Prancey prance prance down the avenue like it's your 10th birthday in equine years.

How to Politely Decline an Invitation to an Airport Lounge or How to Meet New People Without Being Creepy

Take your pretzels elsewhere, fist full of foil: public sex and cameras don't mix. Surveillance is a beautiful woman in heels and a suitcase on wheels in a concourse larger than the town you grew up in. Airports are minor cities, with moving sidewalks and portable art.

They get paraded past you: metal plated wings on lapels, preteens in matching track jackets, red fauxhaux, blue plugs, impractically heavy vintage Samsonites, and, if it's Monday, every third person wearing a dark tie and jacket. If it's Sunday, sunburned dads touting their skinny second wives and their children from his first marriage waving brightly painted alligators on sticks.

Bottled water is an appropriate drink to offer a potential friend, especially in JFK when the AC flicks off or in Dulles during a blizzard.

Look longingly after the "business class" lounge. Remember when your cousin claimed "business class" was over. If you had the extra money to fly first class, you probably had the extra money to rent/own your own damn plane. Remember when your history teacher joked that, whenever you weren't sure what the answer was, just write "rise or fall of the middle class."

Once, you spent the night in the lounge while a major snowstorm buried O'Hare. A woman held her dog over a potted plant. A man doped a cat to slump in its cage. You slept on the floor with dozens of others; woke to strange hair snoring into your chest.

At Hour 15, you start sweating and it smells. 90% of desperation is just boredom in disguise. Hit the green-tiled restroom, the one far away from most of the gates. Take a "wide stance."

Recycled air and watery drinks. The toilet seats spin, replacing plastic with plastic. Autotuned pop wafts above artificial orange. A disembodied voice summons Madison Bennett and Elvira Drum. It's easy to lose someone, even yourself. Page yourself to baggage claim and wait.

How to Enjoy Your Wedding as a Pregnant Bride

White means nothing but night sun in Alaska, where you hurry cold fish down a belt with a knife. This eye-lens is over-focused. Your dress should shimmer from cleavage to knee, but you're covered in fish guts. Smear smelt across your thigh, then cover it with garter.

A baby's inside you. She/he/it is scraping at you with the piece of champagne glass you swallowed almost on accident. She/he/it isn't you. Is the point she/he/it is trying to get across when it kicks your belly into the shape of borrowed blue balloon.

Now say I do for two to too, whose name will be Spring Break or Facebook or Tweet. Let's eat some marzipan birds and some marzipan bees. Saturday brunch, no shellfish or pork. Don't go reaching for anything like a pet. Cats carry disease; you loan yours to your sister. She vies for the kid, but it kicks like a keeper.

How to Cope When Someone Disrespects a Pastime You Are Passionate About

Synchronized swimming at Space Camp, intramural Dungeons and Dragons in Social Dance, playing oboe in French Revolution Reenactment Society, Club for Enthusiasts of Competitive Cricket and Birds of North America—The list of things you didn't do goes on without you.

In the middle of dream-type experience, my roommate gave me a semi-motivational, semi-frustrational kick in the lumbar back: Stop fucking fretting about whether other people would like the things you like. Because, my roommate said, in a mostly unrelated non-dream-type experience, Just look at other people. They're not only not happy, they're not even interesting.

Stage crew captain for the Chess Team Tournament, flag twirler in the Japanese culture meetings, referee of the Yearbook Committee, vice-president of Sisters Against Drunk Texting, equipment manager of the state-champion knitting and crocheting team (Junior Varsity)—You are on ten years of nerve-splay without even a framed certificate of participation to show for it. It is four o'clock in the afternoon and the girl sharing your taxi wants to know just what it is that you do.

Risk it, there in Frank's taxi: text your answer on the palm of her hand. When she blushes, say you'll show her over and over. This is something you do best. Summon up the alphabet: a little A, a little B; here's C now, connecting D's day's dots. Thoughts are for thinkers. Thinking should be a respectable hobby, like personal shopping for the Chief of Police.

How to Quit Smoking or How to Remove Mold Lines from Metal Miniatures

Quit at the state line. At 3:00 sharp. While speeding past armadillo flats. Hacking up purple tenderlung. In an unmarked car. Pretend to get bothered by others' concern. Now is the time for Sunday promise makes. Chew a patch, slap some gum on your arm. Set your head on tangential, remember how one year ago, a plane crashed in the woods and you didn't hear it.

There is a rambling drunk in your voicemail box. He says tinnitus is contagious, it's time to stop trusting government initiatives. You break a window on accident and others act like it's a withdrawal symptom.

Think of your ex: all mouth. Smoke rising from an unarmed house. Admit you'll never quit, but be quiet about how much you love the taste. And blowing smoke in Rambler's face.

State line wavers in heat-haze three cars from border guards. A child bolts from a truck holding a miniature plane. G cars peel out beyond the checkpoint. The plane lands in a tufted tree.

Chainsmoke, listening to border radio: cartel this, illegal that. Surrounded now: child running in fits around your car, guard dogs off leash, smoke from the woods.

Helicopters fluster dust. Tinny airplane cracks a wing. Declare only your best intentions. Lose your passport in the dash.

How to Apply for Unemployment in Texas

Take a number. Enjoy a variety of magazines, cool water from the bathroom sink. Beyond the horizon is a bank account with your name on it. You're waiting in line for Texas to lead you somewhere else.

Dust stains the window. You might be anywhere, waiting for anything you've always wanted. Last month, hot tar and shakes on a roof; the roof caved in; you didn't fall. This is what you get for not falling, this serpentine line and a tangle of chairs.

Stay calm when the man ahead of you shakes his fist, runs to his truck, and returns with one hand in his jacket pocket. Stay calm when six babies start crying in sync. There are words for this. Remember not falling. When they call your number, place your toes on blue tape. A photograph. A list of places you've driven, trucks you've lived in, scars and frayed knots.

There are forms and then there are forms. Use black or blue pen. Press hard, these are triplicates. According to the clock on the side of the clerk's wrist, you've been here for fifteen minutes. It feels more like fifteen hours, you joke, to no one in particular. The vending machine with the Kit-Kat bars and the 4-packs of gum is looking more and more appealing-like. When you were younger, you wanted sex, drugs, and country-western with maybe a bit of Top 40 thrown in to make you not afraid of what was going to happen next. Remember the Alamo? Now your demands are more reasonable, more pathologically pathetic. What kind of human is satisfied with a Kit-Kat bar and a Pepsi, for Chrissake? What kind of person is too tired for a little good old fashioned teenage troublemaking in a federal building?

How to Avoid Making a Bad Situation Worse

(doe yr eyes. bob's yr uncle.

drink saltwater.

pull taffy out of hair w/a mixture from grandmamma.

feather the bottom of beds. compost as much as possible. you are so thorny, you are immune from rosestems.

o tapwater. o fizzy water geyser.

sass back with skirt-lure and hell-prance. ask wrong chess piece to dance until unmentionable

illness gets mentioned at dinner table. pass a peach.
strum cigarettes en route to pawn bob's letter

jacket. spazz out @ waterfront, ice cream and beer in plastic cups, syringes on flotsam.

fuck yea, Americana in the afternoon. give up on waiting for the phone to ring. stretch before running

as far away from your place of origin as the geography of innocent flesh on the bone allows. traffic-

yellow buckeyes will watch out for you. until the end of being young and unbreachable.

o nuclear water swimming home.)

How To Recognize Radiation Sickness

She was carrying her Godzilla-skinned purse.

Indicative of doubledouble toil and trouble.

I didn't know there were so many shades

You're fireburned and cauldron bubbled.

The core gets threatened vis a vi.—

My heart is growing a tail and a second set of fins.

All the eggs lost their hair.

It's @ 1–4 Gy or 100–400 rad.

So that I'm complaining of an acute everything.

Duct tape me to a fainting couch; put it in water like it's a Viking barge.
(Cover in gardenia wreath.)

O, the sweet ionization of my body over the ocean, under the sea.

Roll tide. Roll crib. Roll crumpled newsprint into crimson core, balloon
suits bursting brave last moments

Bottled water litters an island of dismembered buildings.

Dog Saved From Roof

I remember you now.

You were the stranger beside me, waiting in line at the airport. We watched a wall of water crumple cars, bury houses. The airport was made of glass. We watched our city drowning past.

How to Recognize a Breach in History

We hope the dog will lead us to his family.

How to Get Rid of Bruises

Admire the setting sun on your thigh, indolent purple and lemon. At the market, everyone wants to be your guide dog. They intercede when the cashier overcharges. Or, you are the cashier. You overcharge because you're bruised. When someone sets perfect fruit on the conveyer, know they put the bruised fruit back.

Sometimes we are bone-hurting and sometimes we are muscle-hurting and the difference is important but it's not quite clear why. Bury the bruise in a pot of boiling ants.

Skin's a door. She's banging it or you to yesteryear. You live in the basement now. You're getting thinner, swanning your neck. Bruise is the only light you own.

For God's sake, flip the switch. This is an undercover secret. The boiling ants are dancing on the inside of your arm. Some will come to say that this is the point at which you caught that disorderly conduct unbecoming of. So, flick and pick at it.

Get rid of the body of water. Get rid of stepstools and spools of thread threatening Xmas over your cubicle. When she touches you abruptly, bite. Rinse wrists from your girlish daze. There's a goat in the shape of a doctor. She's wearing a hooded glare, but, it's January if she's hooved, shorn, shellacked. Each time you leave, she begs you back.

How to Pretend You Have a Pet or How to Make a Secret Compartment in a Carpet

Weave a flaw into the afternoon. Genie-it up—a terrifying shimmer or 1970's synthetic shag.

Microchip your maiden name. Or, just check the box on the form. Neuter the next three things you see. Become a spot-removing maven.

Choose abandonment from the "free" pile. Inside abandonment is a tiny apartment, equipped with an imaginary urban farmstead. Ask me about my rooftop garden! Those pink flamingoes only look plastic!

Cover the secret compartment with a chainsaw bear. Refer visitors back to the translator on the ground floor. Have them shimmy past shotgun. Wind up downwind upscale chainlink. Free all the mink. Closets are for clothes and heads of the neighborhood association. Jackets are for 1960's girls in gangs.

Remember, pole dancing and throw rugs don't mix. When someone knocks, bark and throw shoes.

Make a fanpage for your mad decorating skills. "Like" everyone's status updates, but don't tell them about the chainsaw bear. People need to discover certain internet ephemera on their own time.

Wait for wooden floorboards to go out of style.

How to Ignore Pain and Feelings

*

Duct tape the cabinet door under the kitchen sink shut to keep bats from flying into the pasta pot on nights your friends are all hanging out together without you.

*

Starve yourself stupid in front of the Lincoln Memorial. And/or read as many biographies as possible.

*

Trigger Warning

*

Have you ever seen a bat up close? It's basically a mouse with wings. It's basically neither cute nor scary.

*

If heat-seeking, assume fetal position.

*

My therapist can beat up your therapist—my therapist is sleeping with your therapist. Hand over your milk money.

*

Tiptoe down hallways listening for lies about your mother. Parse sighs behind lockdown. Look out for leaping lizards. There's no 13th story. The 13th story has no end.

*

Promise someone you love you'll hollow out your innards with tornado gusto so her hands fit cozy-like under your ribscrim. See, you're nothing like she thought you'd be.

*

Marry the last door you ever thought you'd open. Marry the stove. Marry the freezer, and when you kiss, weld tongue to ice: burn. And now the house is burning, and you in it; objects are no more reliable than people. What goes up in flames comes down. Your friends are still at the bar. Text them. Tell them not to save the tiny blue umbrellas.

How to Avoid Drama with Your Best Friend

(friends say fuck you too.
    flag comment as inappropriate.
fish for compliments.
    fugly yourself.
find neon yellow kneepads.
    accept tablescraps or floorcrumbs.
fold your cards if she's the house.
    flame her ex though you full know better.

break in green-tipped shoes.
    break out in fear of saying the wrong thing at the wrong time.
break down in the back seat of lake-bound convertible.
    break up with your sweetheart in the supermarket where she works
    full-time now.
break side-by-side if she's pretending sick again.
    break diagonal if you're still teacher's pet on accident.

polka-dot her stoop in pink-and-silver, girl gang graffiti colors.
    poke.
pace when she asks if you ever lied.
    push when you ride the bus she rides.
pretend-friend her friends on Facebook; spy.
    paint flames on the side of her well-tethered barn.

toe whatever line at whatever time.
    touch toes so ruffles show.
torque her words into arrows; throw.
    tidy up, invite her to tea sip.
throw cup at wall to left of her head.
    tremble. is it over yet.)

How to Get a Job Without a GED or How to Ride a Horse with One Arm

Congenially lipsticked, get appalled by the other beautician-in-training—you're sure she eavesdrops on every occasion. Glower at her mere suggestion of your fall palette. Worry that your smokebreak crew can't tell when you are kidding. Do "irreparable harm" to the right side of the Styrofoam head holding the practice wig. Make halfhearted attempt to receive tuition refund.

Get crafty. Hammer a wooden horse. Rebrand bottled water, claiming it's from Jennifer Aniston's clogged kitchen sink. Sell sips of water from the horse's mouth.

Flick your wrist with gender neutral precision. Win a scholarship to Corporate Coffee Academy; study crop rotation and rudimentary Italian. Get fired when you reveal that a machine pulls the shots.

While waiting tables, learn to assess customers' tip potential. Seat cheapskates in Brittanie's section; she's only working to pay for new skis. Be sure to visit the kitchen off-hours. Load up on groceries, aprons, and knives.

Sign up for internet dating sites. Lure them in with explanations for your distaste of "laughter," "music," and "walks on the beach." Claim you're not looking for a sugar daddy—all the best sugar daddies are the ones who think they're not sugar daddies. Force the term "silver fox" into your unflinching lexicon.

Go on a trip to Aruba or Acapulco. Botox flat feet so flip-flops fit. Get separated from date in starfish-themed restaurant; beg US embassy drone for use of cellphone and/or horse. Straddle drone. Tuck cellphone into pompadour. Ride off into sunset, dating-site-style.

How to Choose a Wedding Cake or How to Practice Non-Attachment

Finger-frost rows of honey roses. Scarify toppers with sugar water. *May your love be indestructible like caketoppers and does anyone object?* Pause for a shift into fourth or fifth dimension.

Clink your own glass and kiss the back of your hand. How you met your outer bride or inner child. Turn off all the lights and shine a flashlight at guests.

Reserve the first dance for your father, who's half-immigrant, half-dead. Request that each guest sing the national anthem of their time zone of origin.

Shred tax receipts and open letters to the Buddha = homemade confetti. Toss a bouquet of poison ivy in the direction of your nemesis, who's crashed the party wearing footie pajamas. Change into footie pajamas because you are your nemesis. Don't see double, see champagne cocktail hour x 2.

Seat guests in a circle while presents are placed under your feet. Read each card aloud: *If you see the Buddha, kill the Buddha.* Ignore the presents, even the coffee and nut grinder combo.

Remember a past lover you forgot to invite. Call her up by a Christian name and explain that the party's almost over, but you will begin it again on her behalf.

How to Reset Your Password

Remember your kindergarten teacher's first pet's maiden name minus the street you grew up on, times the place you met your spouse. This is your drag race name.

Your new password must contain at least one of the following symbols:
&&&&&&&&&&&&&&&&&&&&&&&&&&&

Do not use recognizable combinations of letters, such as HAPPYPANTS or CRUISECONTROL. Remember that computer generated passwords make you look fat.

If you've forgotten your password, answer one of the following security questions in Gaelic:

What is "nice"?
Do you know the way to San Jose?
How many coyote make a flock?

When your email address is hacked and a zombie spams your friends with ads for Canadian drugs, drive to Canada. Take advantage of low, low prices. Return with an accent and a drug-sniffing dog.

There are some things you should never buy online: sedatives for the cats, celebrity artifacts, lube. Never respond to IMs from profiles that use photo stock. Facebook requests from people with over 3000 friends will not make you popular.

All untenured listserv e-mails get filtered through a Nigerian prince in polite need of your immediate assistance. All severe weather updates end with GoogleMap directions to the nearest shelter. All news updates end with predictions of global financial collapse and/or sexual misconduct on the part of Capitalist Royalty.

I went to Craigslist and all I was found was this other roommate. Or Must like cats, but not own any. Electronica enthusiasts a plus. Or, *God grades on the cross, not on a curve.* This means you're in the part of Mississippi with all the light-up church signs. Religions have been surprisingly quick at embracing this digital revolution. Or, *Christ on a Media-Run,* they still make sinners like they used to.

How to Be and Look Like A Mean Girl While in Girl Scouts or How to Make a Bullet Belt

Stitch a counterfeit sash suffused with bilked badges. Sashay in real time into woods. Don't waste your youth—make fire with matches, or, better yet, flamethrowers. Mash burnt marshmallows into bullet pellets; paste to your waist. Wait. Finger pricks = blood sisters or saints.

Code name: Cookie

Code name: Ricochet

Bubble roots and boil stones. Gargle downriver. Show merit with one-hand scout-knotted behind troop leader's back. Pop pseudoephedrine and Vitamin B. Flash concerned forest rangers. Prevalent cure for the common STD involves fleshing out backs with training bra straps.

Code name: Poppy

Code name: Feral

Pitch hissyfit inside of tent. Pitch hissyfit instead of tent. Flick poison ivy prods for progress. Swear unto others there's a bear hiding around campsite. Promote sitting pretty in the face of bestiality and/or danger. Give each other bear hugs.

Code name: Impromptu

Code name: Stacy

Carve loyalty oath into oak trunk. Blindfold potential pledges; spin. Wake numb to pine needles and bird noise nesting. Craft netting from kudzu and flip-flops from bark. Remember to stretch leg and brain muscles, even if you don't think you are going to be hiking all that far.

Code name: Landline

Code name: Merit

Truth-or-dare your troop. What happens in Girl Scouts, stays in Girl Scouts. Make new best friend and dump the old. The bear ended up going over the mountain, but you stayed put. Scold sky for grayline. Skim treeline for planes; take aim. Squirt guns work as well as mace. If you find an empty plane, do not run to the nearest adult.

Code name: Quark

Code name: Lariat

How to Get Over Your Fear of Doing a Cartwheel or How to Give a Feedback Sandwich

1. Compliments mean more legs over your head

2. Skirt doubles as a ruffled top

3. Please is a good beginning

4. No running start for you, young duck!

5. Praise the first and last in line

6. Invest in liminal slow-growth bonds

7. Save caterwaul hours for down o'clock

8. Be grateful strangers knead bread in your breadbox

9. Right foot forward, left foot back

10. Shake. It. All. About.

11. Go team, go west. Time to throw a fit-fest.

12. The coach's reach gets habitually immoderate

13. I know several ways to improve your score—but they're all just this side of unethical

14. Praise Jesus and all other friends of the ref's family!

15. What's this now about a complex carbohydrate?

16. Like the horned and the hoofed, the salted and the sated

17. And you already know how to top the food pyramid

18. Maybe add some flamethrowers? Or just the matching headbands?

19. She still wants to be thrown up

20. Now try it with one hand tied behind your back—

How to Practice Supermarket Checkout Etiquette

Color-code purchases while waiting for the couple in front of you to place a barrier on the moving belt. Read magazines that are dog-eared or about dogs. Comment loudly on each actress's weight or rhinestone collar.

Anything eaten in line is free. This life-rule should not be applied outside of the supermarket.

Decide at the last minute against purchasing any of the perishables in your cart. Stash cheese, zucchini, and tangelos behind candy bars. It's the kindness in you that does everything possible to make the clerks' clean-ups more exciting.

Open a box of tampons. Place one on the belt. Explain to the checker that you only need one. Wink. Point to the button on your jacket that proclaims the day of your cycle.

Dancing to instrumental remixes is acceptable if you drop something made of glass. Paper or plastic—just nod sheepishly.

Answer your phone. Pretend it's POTUS, calling to consult. Say "Yes, Mr. President" several times.

If someone puts meat on the belt, ask them which part of the animal it came from. Blink. Point to the button on your jacket that proclaims your status as a level 4 vegan.

Should you find yourself in line for more than seven minutes, start to pray loudly to invented gods. Sit down on the linoleum and rock yourself back and forth. Try and work in phrases that sound dirty, but aren't. Put your hands on the floor. Stand up. Touch everybody else's food.

Stare when someone enters their PIN. Explain that you're from Ireland or Iceland, and don't understand American math.

If your basket is full, and the person behind you has only one item, tell them to eat it. Or, if the person is full, offer to eat it for them.

How to Stop Saying the Word "Like" or How to Create a D/u/ress Code

Be sure to rehearse at home. Whatever phrase you choose, it should sound natural when someone abducts you from the farmer's market or roller derby practice.

Choose words none of your friends would ever say. Everyone chats about thongs and knitting, but *humidifier* and *celery* are underused. Consider juxtaposing popular words incongruously; for example, *I knit a thong out of celery string after juicing veggies for scented humidifier water.*

Grow your roots out. Switch from black eyeliner to brown. Give up body glitter—even the "clear" kind—it makes people think of strippers and strippers are bad, unless they're tattooless teens working their way thru pre-med.

Don't hesitate to take action when abducted, because one hand over your mouth leads to another. If someone tries to put you in a car, using the word *like* correctly should not be your primary concern.

When in dire need of attention, call out *Fire!* rather than *Help!* or *Rape!* Studies show that innocent ambivalent bystanders are less able to look away from the word fire. Later on, the prosecutors will ask you if you realize that it is equally problematic to shout *Theater!* at a crowded fire.

Act professional, even when dragged behind the stairwell at work. Remember you are a role model. Your duress code should showcase your individual talents and job description. Keep a précis of your goals for the next fiscal quarter in the breast pocket of your powder blue powersuit, wave around like a handkerchief when rescue seems uncertain.

Cleavage is never acceptable. Therefore the word *cleavage* is a good addition to your duress code cache. For example, *My cleavage is, like, totally free range*, is a phrase that does not commonly occur in polite conversation. This is a sure sign that you need help or new clothes.

How to Put High Heels on a Guy While He's Asleep

1.
Make sure this is not a related-to-you-by-blood kind of deal. Cut the tags off, but keep the receipts. I mean, o, yeah, like you're the first person ever to think of subverting the patriarchy.

2.
If only you had taught her how to use the espresso machine correctly, she never would have switched to tea, this whole gender transgression could have been avoided like an Oktoberfest in the midst of a poppy field.

3.
Next time, it's my way or else I'm calling the non-911 *minor* emergency number. If our city even still has one. Because you'll pry these Louboutins from my red, dead fingers.

4.
Find a typewriter. The only way to tell her starts out old-fashioned: tap each key with fierce intent.

> *Dear Darling,*
>
> *We both know you lent me your heels on purpose. Heels feel right on my heels and I move in skirts like I was born to it, codes written inside me, typed. So I'm typing this letter. I'll be out when you get it, downtown drinking coffee or downing shots. Call me when you know what we should do. It's one thing to wake up in heels, and another thing to keep on walking.*

How to Survive a Tornado

If you are over 60, spend 70% of yr waking hours watching the weather channel on behalf of the locations of yr grandchildren and nieces. If you are under 60, spend 70% of yr waking hours contemplating red-rubied feet shriveling under homestead. Think fast, it's a ten alarm. There's no such thing as basements, pick the room with the least number of windows. Go ahead. And pick which one of the 3 Musketeers you could do without, if it came down to that. Update yr Facebook status to read, *OH NOOOOO!* Have fun watching others guess as to just what exactly you're no-ing. Give up on the pets; hope that nature will override their nurture, they'll come back once you stop cowering in the bathtub, under a mattress. If you have children, stash them in the top-load washer: the safest place.

In Miami, hurricanes: alligators wrapped around palmettos. In Seattle, earthquakes: cracked air traffic control towers and shop fronts shedding sheets of brick.

Most dangerous of all is driving to the store. Take a moment of silence to remember the Manzettis, ex-next-door neighbors. Last week the family ambled to the grocery for a block of cheese. Their SUV flipped over on Hobash, rolled into traffic. Six blocks from home.

Remember the Manzettis' dog. If you own a bike, take a right onto Hobash. Park your bike by the side of the road. Walk into the woods like you know where you're going. Find the nest before you find the dog.

How to Prevent Malaria When You're Traveling

The locals are restless, wrestling with someone else's demons, no you cannot take a picture of the cross on the forehead of a chupacabra-type creature. There are rules; the embassy is either very far away or very blown to smithereens.

Send reassuring postcards home, *Everything's fine! Learning a lot about the customs of other people! Miss you!* Cover yourself up more than necessary, try to come off as teenage boy. Or, at least, as ambiguously European.

Cut your thumb on accident washing dishes in the hostel that's not really a hostel. Bleed for twenty minutes. Then allow the night manager to use superglue. Drink lots of quinine water. Slip a pile of large orange beads under your pillow.

Dream of night shift, machinery rumbling, speaking in tongues. Wake up in someone's backpack, stuffed. Or walking the edge of a cliff, peering over, wondering how many virgins the volcano devoured.

Drink fizzy orange lunch and slather nutbutter. Tiptoe past sneezes. Breathe through your hands. If you fall in love while traveling, be sure to use a fake name and fake country of origin. Anyone might be a spy. Above all, no American flags on your lapel. Some countries see red, white, and blue and imagine bombs falling in a shower unlike any Fourth of July your imagination might concoct.

When you marry the seventeenth stranger you meet, exchange buttons instead of rings.

Stay away from windows: you're allergic to broken glass. Pack light. Carry a pocketknife. Whatever you do, don't steal someone's baby. Pirates are easily dissuaded by setting the ship's left flounce on fire.

How to Appreciate an Obese Family Member

Scarves are appropriate for any occasion. For men, a necktie in neutral colors. Swedish uncle looks lovely in blue.

Feed children three meals a day, arranged chromatically on crockery. Portions should be finger-length; wait until rice cools before measuring.

Invent fictitious childhood memories: swim camp, dance camp, Bible camp. Invent first counselor crush at anarchy camp, flag burning s'mores.

Please and *thank you* should be handwritten in illegible script, vowels missing to deify family biography.

Mismatched socks require an intervention. Criss-crossing interventions take time away from food preparation, so be sure no one's planning an intervention for you.

Holiday conversation should be limited to: food, TV, cute animal videos, distant cousins' drug problems (not yours). Sass back if anyone comments on your parallel parking. Remind them that you learned to park in a major urban center: Philly or Miami, you can't remember. It was years ago, and you were too young. Swedish uncle wanted you to learn in case he keeled over at the wheel, which he did, as you drove slowly into a fence.

Speak fake Swedish to young cousins. Tell them good Swedes wear candles in their hair. Out of the singed cinch of hair ribbon and ash explain that candle bearing is a test of pureheartedness.

Sing the wrong hymn in church while practicing kegels. Pour equal measures of cardamom and coffee into the rickety plastic pot.

At niece's graduation, mark your face in her favorite colors. She will pretend to be embarrassed, but that's what family is good for. Stand on tiptoe until her name's called, then leave conspicuously in a newer car.

Throw fit in the lake on the grandmother's Wisconsin property. It was your turn to be Marco to the other cousins' Polo, you just know it. Act surprised when grandfather whacks you on the butt with a gaping trout. You should know better than to act less than your 100 years.

When long-lost son shows up on doorstep, allow him the couch but not the guest room. Until he can pass a DNA test, all bets are off. Remember your ex's warnings about hookers without hearts of gold. It's snowing unseasonably though, and you could really use someone to shovel your Cadillac out of the driveway.

If the plague hits, disavow the patri-line. This isn't feminism, it's survival. Any heirloom is a weapon if you hold it right.

How to Remain Unchanged by Fame

Every mirror houses imaginary people. Decline edible underwear unless the wrapper's intact. The real you should always be present at birthdays. Say: I love myself because I am me.

If the heads give you any grief, remember, you are a Dior in a McQueen wrapped in a von Furstenberg, fucking your way out of a designer paper bag that's not yours, but it is, because it looks great on you, baby.

Everyone's famous to their dog, anyway. Scratch your arms, pretending cat. Clarify which paraphernalia performs. Time orgasms to the village clock.

Flip thru and thru. It's rosebud gathering time. Set about rearranging the mirrors back to the way you like them.

Dry-worry, seed-worry, worry-worry. Count to twenty as you wash your hands. Sleep on the floor, newsprint for pillow. If your face is the headline, recycle your snout.

Tumblr full of goat's milk mixed with vodka. Whatever happened to—? Avoid the checkout lines in the supermarket. Try and fall in love for real this time.

Tattoo your wife's name on your wrist, intertwined with abstract designs: no more guessing or rumpus mistakes! Flagellate chest with chain grocery baguette.

Set a dark pair over your eyes. Drop habits like bad luck hats.

Turn on the TV, wait for your face to float into view, your O mouth to open. O to come out. O is for lonely, bluescreen burnout. Soft burn of the boom brushing your body.

Retire kissyface, Rolodex, hexes. Here's how to hail a cab in a minor city: call first. You'll make friends faster with a dog or a baby attached to your waist with a retractable leash.

How to Stop Thinking that Accepting Help is a Sign of Weakness

1. Stitch an invisible dress

2. In a beige wallpapered tone

3. Assure that you will compensate

4. Tuck Teflon blouse into slack-slimming slacks

5. Laughforce at every fat dyke joke

6. Offer to buy a year's supply of wrapping paper for the martial arts raffle

7. In the shape of a favor, please

8. Fix the chandelier the charity broke

9. Avert raised eyebrows

10. Water the soup

11. Give away your favorite trinket

12. Pick up fault where he/she dropped it

13. It's nothing really

14. Drop her hand

15. Tip 110%

16. Which set of flatware expresses respect

17. Knit mouth shut

18. Nod, hair swaying in pleasing fashion

19. No starrynight walks

20. Cross legs, no showoff

How to Picnic in a Graveyard or How to Get Your Enemy to Like You Romantically

Follow me into the mausoleum. There are as many sorts of sex as ghosts. Here's longspanned whisper, biting spar, manic compassion, recreational slough.

We're rusty girls, pre-rot. Doing it tombstone-style on slab and marble. We mean well, maybe. Don't say *enemy*, say *secret Santa* or *running buddy*.

Undo latch, and spread. Baskets beg reach, racetrack red-checkered flag unfurling over plastic peonies and Everett Smith. Crumbs scramble mismatched maps back to the gate, ornate with nest and ribboned wreath.

Practice embalming on day-old bread. I want you to prepare my body when I die. Place pennies on my eyes to lockdown mourning. Shellac a lock of hair in a locket keyed to your chest.

I'll find new pleasures dressed in dirt. You'll stay rooted to that job you hate, three cats on the sill in a studio apartment.

Take me into the hypnotherapeutic buzz. There are as many sorts of ghosts as sex. Here's a window-trussed, scold-hard, pre-slated mechanical embraceage.

We're psycho in white, pre-analysis. Doing it Freud-style on velvet chaise lounge. They mean well, maybe. Don't say *girlfriend*, say *roommate* or *crew co-captain*.

Redo this patch, then dread. Buckets demand withdrawal, pilgrim black-stripe rug rolled under natural knick-knacks and a man of few words. Pieces orderly like matched globes move forward from the door, plain with broken egg and branch.

Become a natural at decomposing eternal treasurebox. You want me to unprepare your spirit-section for when you get back to life. Displace dollars off your mouth to unlock unmitigated celebration. Melt the eyelashes and fingernails out of the amber rings on king-finger.

You'll lose old pain undressed in cloud. I'll leave, uprooted in that leisure I love, no dogs in the basement of the castle-sized world.

How to Regift a Present

Tie it to your wrist so you're the gift.

Make an arm-bow. Shimmer.

You're beautiful, and you deserve this.

If it's the thought that counts, color me thoughtfilled.

      (in exchange for sex, lawn care, or pet sitting)

Pianos aren't allowed on the seventh floor.

If the gift is a live animal, be sure to punch holes in the sides of the box. Live animals should not be mailed, but sent via courier, which is expensive and can take up to one week.

I never keep receipts!

We think alike!

      (this halved but satiated holiday)

Every state has its own rules about regifting. Be sure to familiarize yourself with section 8.1 of Appendix C.

      (breaking glass, acting like it doesn't bother you)

Not what I was promised, but a promise I kept.

I mean it; you take it. You know you want it.

Ignore monogrammed initials, or say it's part of the design, your new pet name for her.

How to Convince a Shy Person to Be Your Valentine or How to Make a Heart-Shaped Pumice Candle Holder

Fold red paper in half.
Tear seam,

watch livestream
bald eagles

high above Iowa.
Hearts are just circles

with pointy chins.
Once, a whole squirrel

bled into the nest.
Think fast, he said;

aimed at my chest.
Love looks violent

in seventh grade.
Now wax, handmade,

and a scientist's
camera. X =

kisses in texts
sent from trains.

O = left ring
finger burn,

unexpected turnabout
is fair play.

Instant poof
for the buttons

on the woman
side of the shirtdress.

I keep a stuffed
flower in my traincase

for the whole
stretches of middle

in the birdsong-
less Oklahoma night.

How to Build a Remote Controlled Robot

Don't touch it when it's sleeping. It will honk like a cross between a goose and a children's bicycle. If it wakes all the way up, give it dresses—jeans will just let it in on how fat it is getting.

Everyday, it will thank God for Helvetica. The entire state of Florida is coming for the two of you. We're way past our pitchfork phase.

You got the idea after it claimed the street behind your house smelled like honeysuckle. When you knew full well there was no nose-function built in.

Note what's gone missing around the house: vibrator, toaster, fondue pot, gum. Don't say anything when a bubbling vat of gum appears family-style at Sunday dinner.

Introduce it to the refrigerator. Listen from the living room as hums converge. When you knew full well there was no love-function built in.

Thereafter, jealousy toward other appliances may be exploited for the purpose of home improvements. Pay close attention to the dishwasher and oven, which touch the refrigerator on either side.

Leave straight-edge razors out by its favorite Adirondack porch chair. Watch secret-like from behind the topiary.

Consider a hyphenated surname. "Remote" sounds dignified attached to your own.

How to Stop Being in Love With a Person You'll Never Meet

Tell the birds nesting in the eaves that it's over. Tell them to flutter tall grass in Ohio. She is all Ohio now, wind lifting the cuffs of her sleeves. You imagine her wrists rubbed red from washing, doctor or mother or cutter or saint. Your *no* is a *note* tied to *nothing* and *no one*, easy to swallow with thimbles of gin.

Absence is a promise best kept to oneself. A paradigm, the paradigm of numbed planning. She is still needlessly equidistant between the coasts. O, say it's for the best three times fast then put on your housecoat and spin till the birds fling south for what's going to seem like a very long time.

The rubbed red will get everywhere soon enough.

How to Feel Confident with Your Special Talents

How to Open an Umbrella. How to Treat Cat Anorexia. How to Eject from a Runaway Kite. How to Make Thin Lips Thick with Three Shades of Lipstick. How to Film Home Movies in Someone Else's Home.

Confidence shows in the swirl of your skirt when you witness a postal worker fending off a raccoon: How to Treat Wounds.

Some people, for example, are talented at sex. Some people are talented at composing original songs on the accordion. Some people have no talent whatsoever, but their lack of talent makes other talents seem grander by comparison.

How to Bake Gluten-Free Banana Bread. How to Break the Glass Ceiling at Work when You Work in a Glass Factory. How to Fight Fair in High Heels and/or Flats.

If you smile while you enact your special talent, confidence will rise from your toes and extend beyond your hair extensions.

How to Design an Insignia Your Whole Family Will Admire. How to Date a Closeted Coworker. How to Avoid Giving Out Halloween Treats.

How to Digest Cherries. How to Paint Over Big Mistakes on Your Public Works of Art. How to Drug a Hamster. How to Get Along with Your Friend's Brother's Wife. How to Jump Up and Down Like a 5 Year Old. How to Sleep in a Twin Bed in a Motel in Hattiesburg, Mississippi. How to Pep-Up a Martini. How to Poison a Well. How to XXX. How to Slip on a Banana Peel. How to Arrange Your Record Collection in Alphabetical Order. How to Dervish. How to HowtoHowtoHow. How to Sign a Letter

of Resignation. How to Point the Finger at Someone Else. How to
Ballerina Dip. How to Duck and Cover in Friendly Fire Situations. How to
[read: file error]. How to Double-cross Your Tap Dancing Partner. How to
Make Out Like a Bandit.

Acknowledgments/Notes

Quotation in "How to Avoid Making a Bad Situation Worse" — Charles Bernstein "Sign Under Test," *Michigan Quarterly*, vol. XLI, no. 4, Fall 2002.

Quotation in "How to Stop Saying the Word "Like" or How to Create a D/u/ress Code" — church sign in Mississippi, as related in a text message from Sarah McClung.

"How to Build a Remote-Controlled Robot" appeared in Sad Robot Books—Special Screenprint Edition: Poems About the Sad Robot Sculpture (ed. and designed by Greg Houser).

"How to Take Action when You Lose Sight of Your Child at an Amusement Park," "How to Avoid Drama with Your Best Friend," "How to Make a Meal of One Color, or How to Stop Coworkers from Stealing Your Food," and "How to Stop Being in Love With a Person You'll Never Meet" appeared on the Richard Hugo House blog.

"How to Calculate the Value of Scrap Gold" and "How to Apply for Unemployment in Texas" appeared in *Consequence*.

"How to Convince a Shy Person to Be Your Valentine or How to Make a Heart Shaped Pumice Candle Holder," "How to Earn a Legitimate Living Working from Home," and "How to Donate Your Body to Science" appeared in *South Dakota Review*.

"How to Be and Look Like A Mean Girl While in Girl Scouts or How to Make a Bullet Belt" appeared in *Fairy Tale Review* (The Grey Issue).

"How to Do the Cha Cha," "How to Cheat at Poker," and "How to Climb a Ladder Safely" appeared in *Diode Poetry Journal*.

"How to Ensure No One Argues when Playing Princess Party Games or How to Stop Misbehaving in Public" appeared in *Sixth Finch*.

"How to Avoid Leaving DNA at a Scene or How to Descend a Staircase Gracefully," "How to Draw an Accurate Mental Map of the World," "How to Ride an Icelandic Horse," "How to Be Friends With a Lesbian" appeared in *The Jet Fuel Review*.

"How to Politely Decline an Invitation to an Airport Lounge or How to Meet New People Without Being Creepy" appeared in *Revolution House*.

Daniela:

Thanks to my fellow scribes and friends at University of Alabama for helping me write through the aftermath of an EF4 tornado. Shout outs to Katie Berger, Pia Simone Garber, Breanne LeJeune, and Sarah McClung for their generosity, patience, and willingness to deal with what the not-quite-dead squirrel the kitten dragged in. Much love to Bob Berry, who taught me how to use the internet back when the internet was only for scientists and other nerds. And, of course, special thanks to Carol Guess for inspiration, collaboration, and friend/mentorship.

Carol:

Thanks to Suzanne Paola, Debra Salazar, and my colleagues at Western Washington University.

Special thanks to Elizabeth J. Colen, Alison Fitton, Heather Franklin, Gerry Guess, and Daniela Olszewska.

Carol and Daniela:

Thanks to Amy Freels, Sarah McCarry, Danielle Pafunda, and Kathleen Rooney.

Corinne May Botz generously shared ongoing inspiration and the perfect cover image.

Elizabeth J. Colen provided brilliant editorial and creative advice.

Diane Goettel and all at Black Lawrence Press offered invaluable editorial insight, guidance, and excitement about our project.

Our deepest gratitude to the writers, editors, and publishers of wikiHow for teaching us how to collaborate.